TEACH YOUR KID ABOUT TAME ANIMALS

[ZHINGOORA BOOKS]

CONTENTS

THE HARE.

I suppose you have all seen a Hare, and perhaps many of you have helped to eat one. The Hare is a very timid animal, running away on the least alarm; but, poor fellow, he is too often caught by the dogs and killed, notwithstanding his swift running. It is rather difficult to tame Hares, but there is a very amusing account of three, named Puss, Tiney, and Bess, written by the poet Cowper, who kept them for some time, and one day you shall read about them. The colour of the Hare in this country is usually brown, but white Hares are found in very cold countries. The Hare does not burrow

like the rabbit, but
makes a kind of
nest called its form.

THE GOAT.

The Goat ranks in general usefulness next to the sheep, and as a domestic animal is very valuable. His chief pleasure seems to consist in climbing from [5]one rock to another, for which amusement his hoofs are well adapted. The milk of the Goat is sweet and nourishing, and is made into cheese by the mountaineers, who also eat his flesh, which is rather tough. His skin is made into the materials called morocco leather, and vellum; and that of the young animals, the kids, is used to make the best kinds of gloves. The hair of some species of Goats is soft and fine, and is woven

into shawls of
beautiful texture.

THE COW.

Cows are very
useful to mankind,

in supplying them with milk from which both butter and cheese are made. Their young ones are called calves, and the flesh of calves is veal. A good Cow will give about fifteen or more quarts of milk a day, but much depends upon the quality of the pasture she feeds upon. Her age is told by her horns; after she is three years old a ring is formed every year at the root of the horn, so that by counting the number of circles, her age may be exactly known. Cows are sometimes prettily marked with black, brown, and yellow spots, and, as they lie scattered about

a green meadow,
add much to the
charms of a
landscape.

THE SHEEP.

The Sheep is found in every
quarter of the globe, and is

one of the most profitable animals that mankind possesses. His flesh is eaten by the inhabitants of all nations, and, as you know, is called mutton. The wool of the Sheep is very valuable, and most of our clothing is made from it: that produced by the breed called Merino sheep is particularly fine, and fetches a high price. The skin is also of service, and forms covers for many of your school-books. Sheep-washing and shearing are busy times for the farmer, and are very interesting sights. Young sheep are called lambs—you have often seen the gentle little things skipping about in the meadows.

THE DORMOUSE.

In some places people call this little animal "the Sleeper," because he lies in a torpid state through the long winter and spring, until the weather becomes quite warm. He builds his nest in an old hollow tree, or beneath the bushes, and during the summer lays up a great quantity of nuts or acorns for his winter provender. Dormice rarely come out, except[10]at night, passing the day in a solitary manner in their cells, which they manage to make very comfortable by linings of moss. Dormice are about the size of the common mice, only more bulky, and of a reddish brown colour.

The American Dormouse is a more beautiful animal, striped down the back, and much resembling the squirrel in his habits.

_____

THE ASS.

Is the most patient of all quadrupeds, and, although thought by many to be the most stubborn, he is not really so, but is both active and willing if well treated. Donkeys are generally badly used by their masters, and you cannot go far without seeing one with his skin

End of the book.